D.I.Y. DOLLHOUSE

D.I.Y. Dollhouse

BUILD AND DECORATE A TOY HOUSE USING EVERYDAY MATERIALS

Alexia Henrion

Princeton Architectural Press

New York

Princeton Architectural Press
A McEvoy Group company
37 East 7th Street, New York, NY 10003
202 Warren Street, Hudson, NY 12534
Visit our website at www.papress.com

First published in Switzerland in 2015 by Haupt Bern under the title *Villa Obstkiste*
© 2015 Haupt Bern

For Haupt Bern:
Photos, illustrations, and design concept:
Alexia Henrion, Hamburg, Germany
Design and layout: Daniela Vacas, Bern, Switzerland
Editing: Petra Puster, Niederpöcking, Germany

For Princeton Architectural Press:
Translator: Jane Wolfrum
Project Editor: Nicola Brower
Designer: Mia Johnson

Special thanks to: Janet Behning, Nolan Boomer, Abby Bussel, Tom Cho,
Barbara Darko, Benjamin English, Jenny Florence, Stan Guderski, Jan Cigliano Hartman,
Susan Hershberg, Lia Hunt, Valerie Kamen, Simone Kaplan-Senchak, Jennifer Lippert,
Kristy Maier, Sara McKay, Eliana Miller, Wes Seeley, Rob Shaeffer, Sara Stemen, Paul Wagner,
and Joseph Weston of Princeton Architectural Press —Kevin C. Lippert, publisher

Library of Congress Cataloging-in-Publication Data
Names: Henrion, Alexia, 1984– author.
Title: DIY dollhouse : a recycling activity book for young architects and
furniture designers / Alexia Henrion.
Other titles: Villa Obstkiste. English
Description: First edition, English edition. | New York : Princeton
Architectural Press, 2017. | "First published in Switzerland in 2015 by
Haupt Bern under the title Villa Obstkiste."
Identifiers: LCCN 2017002770 | ISBN 9781616896072 (alk. paper)
Subjects: LCSH: Dollhouses. | Refuse as art material. | Handicraft.
Classification: LCC TT175.3 .H4613 2017 | DDC 745.592/3—dc23
LC record available at https://lccn.loc.gov/2017002770

contents

Preface - 7

Before You Begin - 8

11
HOUSE

Building Instructions - 15

19
LIVING ROOM

Fireplace - 32

Armchair No. 1 - 34

Coffee Table - 36

Sofa - 38

Television - 40

43
BATHROOM

Vanity - 56

Toilet - 58

Bathtub - 60

Hanging Shelves - 62

Washing Machine - 64

67
TEENAGER'S BEDROOM

Daybed - 80

Desk Chair - 82

Display Cabinet - 84

Armchair No. 2 - 88

91
CHILDREN'S BEDROOM

Desk - 104

Lamp No. 1 - 106

Bunk Bed - 108

Swing - 110

Box - 112

115
KITCHEN

Stove & Oven - 128

Bucket & Mop - 130

Sink Unit - 132

Refrigerator - 134

Radio - 136

139
BEDROOM

Wardrobe - 148

Picture Frame - 150

Cradle - 152

Bedside Table & Lamp No. 2 - 154

Double Bed - 156

159
PATIO

Sun Umbrella - 168

Whirlpool - 170

Chairs - 172

Acknowledgments - 176

PREFACE

This book is for all children who like to craft things and enjoy playing make-believe and expressing their creativity. The idea behind it is to create something without having to buy any materials. You can build a whole house from things that you have at home or can get for free in various stores. *D.I.Y. Dollhouse* is all about recycling, reusing garbage, and repurposing disposable products. Before you just throw away another old T-shirt, consider if you can still craft something with it. Before you put your empty yogurt container in the trash, wash it out and make something beautiful out of it. This way you save money, protect the environment, and have a lot of fun to boot!

On the following pages, you will find many suggestions for making furniture for your dollhouse out of disposable products. Not all of the items featured within this book have building instructions, since some of them are self-explanatory. Moreover, I am sure that you will come up with a lot of great ideas of your own for making furniture and fixtures.

Some of the instructions are perhaps a bit complicated or may require special tools that you are not familiar with. In these cases, ask your mother, father, or an older brother or sister if they can help you. You will see that the more you make with the material you have collected, the more of your own ideas you will have.

Have fun building and playing with your own D.I.Y. dollhouse!

BEFORE *you* BEGIN

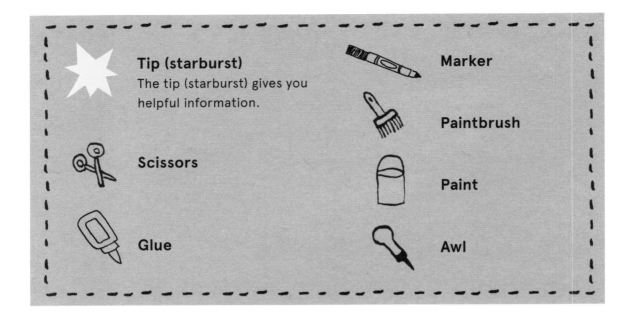

Tip (starburst)
The tip (starburst) gives you helpful information.

Scissors

Glue

Marker

Paintbrush

Paint

Awl

Before you begin building your dollhouse, it is worthwhile to look around your house and see if you can find the materials listed below, with which you can build some amazing things.

- **empty boxes** (of matches, lightbulbs, medications, chocolates, food)
- **empty, rinsed plastic containers and bottles** (from yogurt, cream cheese, and juice)
- **various lids** (screw-on lids, crown caps)
- **empty, rinsed small drink cartons** (from milk, chocolate milk, or juice)
- **colorful paper** (from chocolates or old magazines)
- **old, discarded clothing**
- **large, sturdy boxes** (pizza or shoe boxes)
- **ribbons, strings, and beads**
- **toothpicks, wooden skewers, and drinking straws**

But before you get going, make sure to ask your parents if you are really allowed to use these things. It is also a good idea to keep your eyes open when you are in a restaurant or supermarket, or on your way to preschool or school. You can often find great things, such as little creamer containers, branches, nice candy wrappers, or popsicle sticks.

Always ask your parents if you are allowed to pick these things up and take them with you. If the items you collect are dirty, you must wash them thoroughly—and then your hands too, of course!

Once you have gathered materials, look around your house to see what tools you have. You will probably find glue, paintbrushes, and scissors in your craft drawer. You will also need paint to give some color to your containers and boxes. Oil-based paint provides the

best coverage, but it contains solvents. Therefore, you should always make sure there is good ventilation when you are painting. Even if you use oil-based paint, you usually have to paint twice. Unfortunately, this type of paint cannot be washed out of clothes. So it is a good idea to wear a painting smock over your clothes.

Of course, you can also use other types of paint, such as poster paints or acrylic paints. However, the latter do not cover up the writing on boxes and containers very well, even if you apply multiple coats of paint. It is best to ask an adult which type of paint you should use.

If you do not have an awl to make holes, you can also use a nail and a rubber mallet. Press the tip of the nail against the place where you want to make a hole and then hit the head of the nail with the rubber mallet. Whenever you are not sure, always ask an adult to help you.

Sometimes you have to think outside the box to achieve your goals! Use your imagination and be creative, and you can do anything!

HOUSE

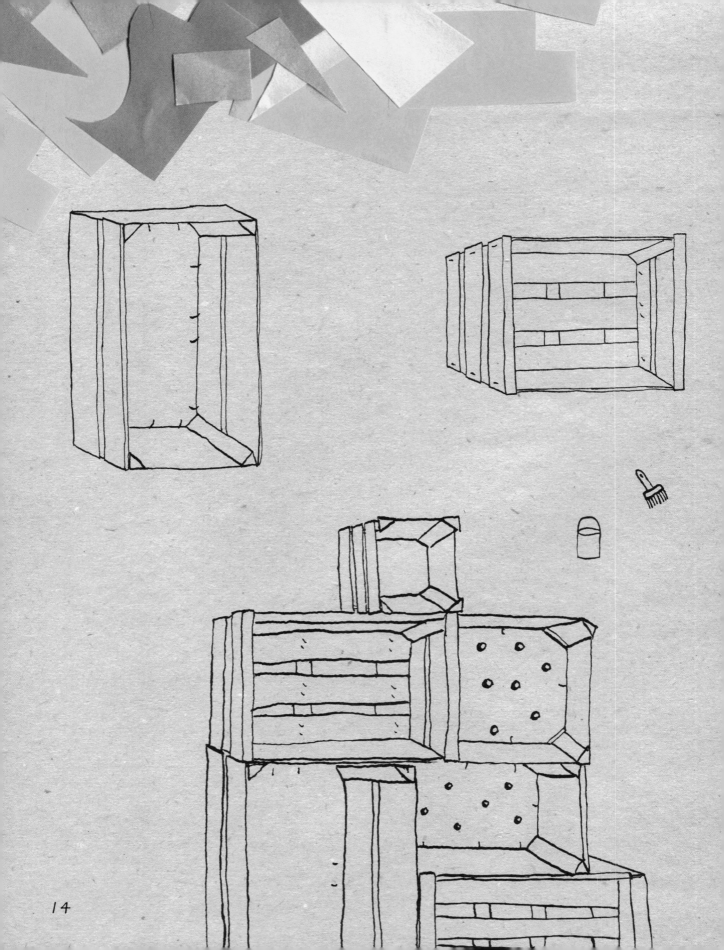

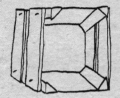

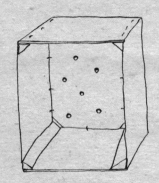

HOUSE

BUILDING INSTRUCTIONS

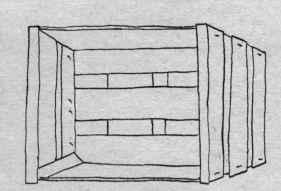

You can usually get crates in various sizes from the supermarket or at fruit and vegetable stands for free. Just ask the salesperson if you can have a few. Often they also have small wooden boxes in which flowers and bulbs are sold. These will also work well for your house.

HOUSE

To build your house, you need crates or wooden boxes. The number of crates depends on how many rooms you want your house to have. The crates you collect will probably be different sizes. Think about which size is best suited for which room before you begin working on them. If you like, you can paint the crates on the inside and outside. You can also cover the walls with giftwrap to create wallpaper.

Use cardboard to cover the floors of the rooms and glue fabric to it, to make it look like carpet. Next decorate the interior of the rooms. You will find a lot of tips and instructions for making furniture and other items on the following pages. Finally, think about how you want to arrange the rooms on top of and next to one another to make the house. Then glue them together with hot glue.

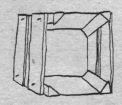

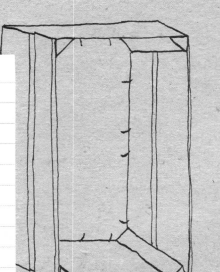

Materials
· (fruit) crates
· giftwrap
· cardboard
· pieces of fabric

Tools
· scissors
· glue
· pencil
· paint
· paintbrush
· painting smock
· hot glue gun

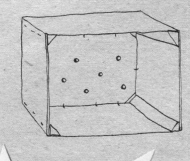

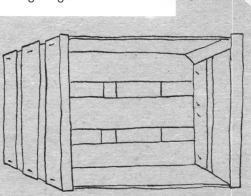

Ask an adult to help you when you are ready to assemble your house. First try a few different layouts before you glue everything together.

LIVING ROOM

23

26

BUILDING INSTRUCTIONS

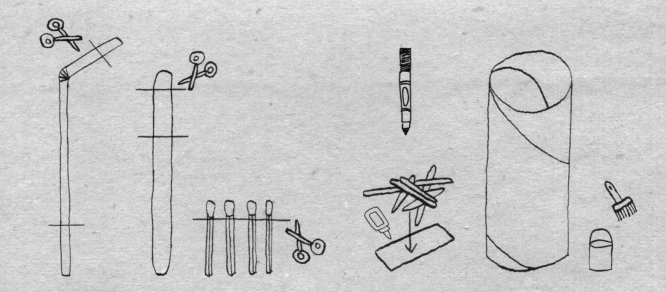

FIREPLACE + CHIMNEY PIPE

To make the chimney pipe, take a flexible drinking straw and cut a little piece off the top and bottom with the scissors. Now cut a small piece from the popsicle stick as shown above. Cut off the heads of a few matchsticks. Glue the matches crisscross on your piece of popsicle stick. You can also color the pile of matches with red and yellow markers to make it look as if the wood is burning.

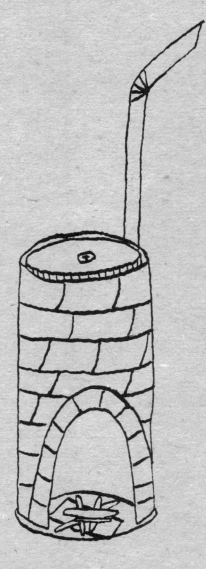

Materials
- flexible drinking straw
- popsicle stick
- matchsticks
- empty toilet paper roll
- large plastic lid (with the same diameter as the toilet paper roll)
- cardboard

Tools
- scissors
- glue
- pencil
- paint
- paintbrush
- painting smock
- markers

CHIMNEY

Now cover your toilet paper roll with paint, inside and out. When it is dry, cut out an oval opening at the bottom. Then glue it to a round piece of cardboard and glue the fire inside the hearth. Put some glue on the outer edge of the lid and insert it into the top of the toilet paper roll. At the same time, slip in the straw between the lid and the toilet paper roll to make the chimney pipe. Finally, you can draw a brick pattern on your chimney with a black marker.

You can find large lids on juice bottles. Paint the lid and straw the same color as your chimney to make everything match.

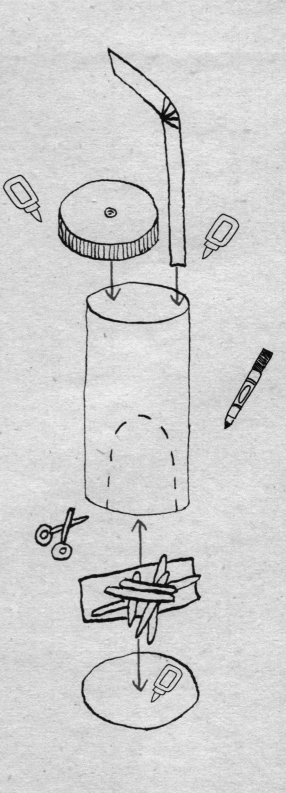

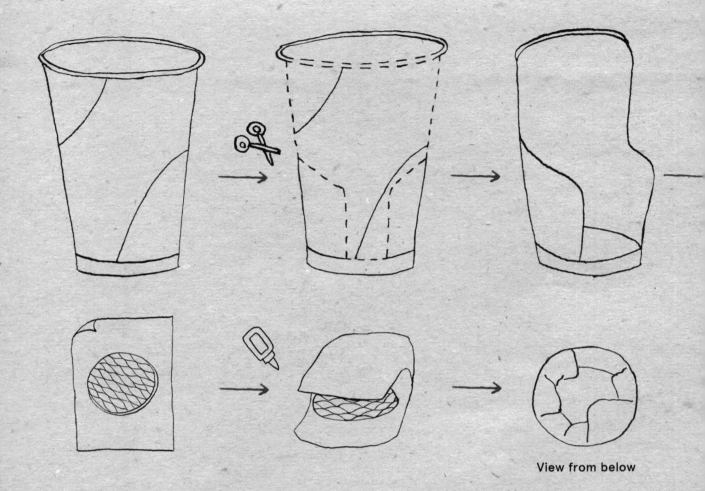

View from below

ARMCHAIR NO. 1

To make this armchair you need a paper cup. Cut it on the dotted line, as shown above (top row of illustrations). Now spread glue on the inside and outside of your armchair and wrap the piece of fabric around it. There will probably be a few creases but that does not matter. Do try, though, to have as few creases on the front of the chair as possible and glue the overlapping fabric together at the back of your armchair. If there is still some fabric sticking out, simply cut it off.

Materials
· paper cup
· 2 pieces of fabric
· round cotton pad

Tools
· scissors
· glue
· pencil

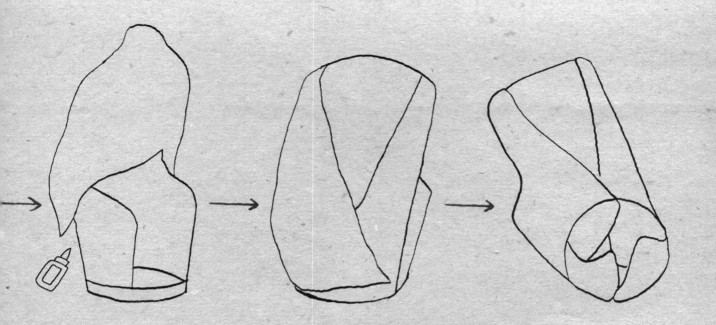

SEAT CUSHION

To make the armchair more comfortable, take a round cotton pad, place it in the center of a small piece of fabric, brush it with glue, and wrap the fabric around it. Try to have creases on only the underside here too.

When the glue on the armchair and cushion has dried completely, you can place the cushion with the smooth side up on the seat of your armchair.

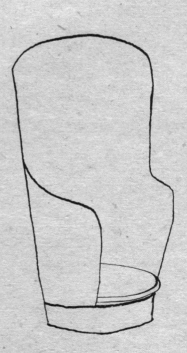

APPLE JUICE

plain yogu
2% fat

COFFEE TABLE

For the base of the table, you need a brown plastic juice bottle. Cut off the upper part of the bottleneck, as shown in the top left picture opposite. You can leave the lid on or throw it away. It doesn't matter.

For the tabletop, you need a large yogurt container. Cut off the lower part, i.e., the bottom of the container, and paint it. When the tabletop is dry, simply flip it over and glue it to the cut bottleneck.

Materials
- brown plastic juice bottle
- large yogurt container

Tools
- scissors
- glue
- pencil
- paint
- paintbrush
- painting smock

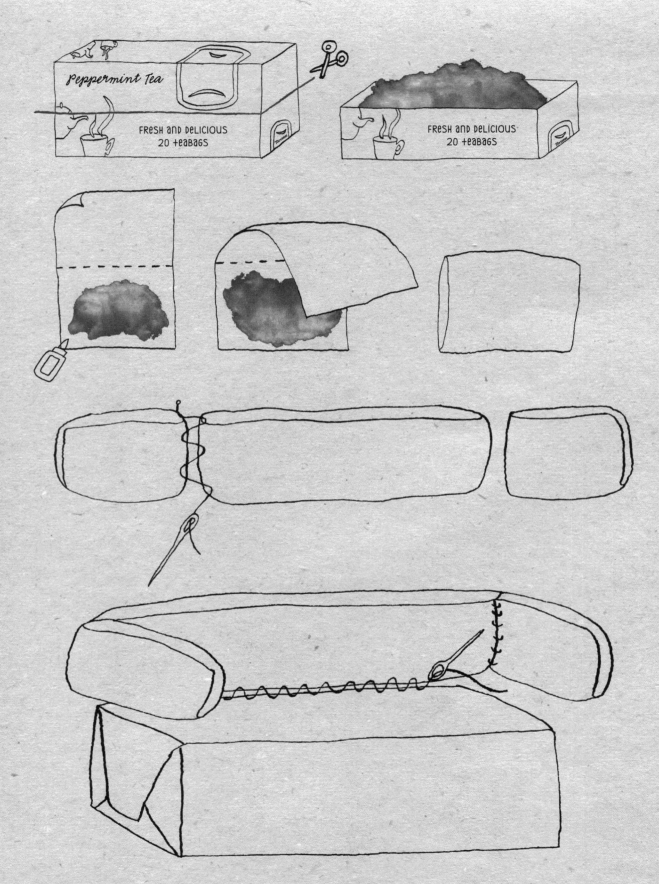

Peppermint Tea

FRESH AND DELICIOUS
20 TEABAGS

FRESH AND DELICIOUS
20 TEABAGS

38 ~ SOFA

Materials
- box
- cotton fluff
- piece of fabric
- thread

Tools
- scissors
- glue
- pencil
- needle

SOFA SEAT

Take your box, cut it in half (along the red line as shown in the top left picture opposite), and fill the lower part with cotton. Now cut a square piece out of your fabric, place the box on it, and wrap it like a present. Glue the edges together on the sides. This is the seat of your new sofa.

Get help from an adult with the sewing.

BACK + ARMRESTS

Now on to the sofa back and armrests: Cut two rectangular pieces of roughly the same size from the fabric (for the armrests), as well as another somewhat longer piece (for the back). Make sure the armrests and back are the right size to fit on your box. Fold each piece of fabric in the middle so that you can see how much cotton you need for the filling. Place the cotton on the fabric and put some glue on the outer edges. Then fold over the other side and press the edge down firmly. When the glue on the seat, back, and armrests is dry, sew the arms to the back and then sew the back and armrests to the seat.

If you do not have any black glossy paper at home, look for pages in magazines that have black areas and simply cut out a piece.

TELEVISION

Take your box and paint it gray. Glue the black glossy paper in the middle of the front. This will be the screen. Now glue the four beads on below the screen to serve as knobs. Finally, draw some speakers on the left and right of the screen with the marker.

Materials
· box
· 4 small beads
· black glossy paper

Tools
· scissors
· glue
· pencil
· paint
· paintbrush
· painting smock
· marker

BATHROOM

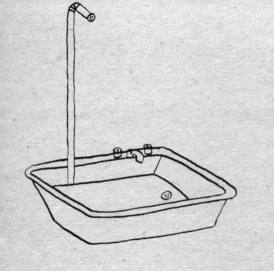

BATHROOM

BUILDING
INSTRUCTIONS

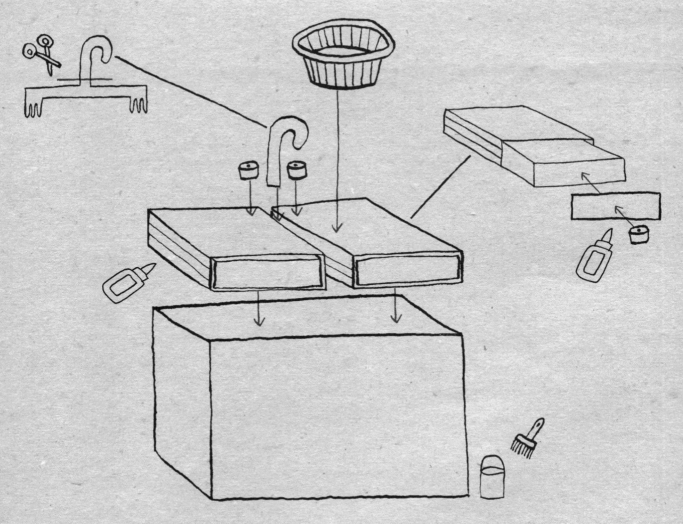

FAUCET &
DRAWERS

First, paint the box and the two matchboxes
in a pretty color. While they dry, you can
work on the faucet. For this you need a small
plastic hanger, like the ones that are used
to display socks in a store. As shown above,
cut off the rounded hook from the rest of
the hanger. Then cut small rectangles out of
your colored paper, glue them to the front
of the matchbox drawers as decoration, and
glue a bead onto each drawer as the handle.

It is best to give
the matches from
the matchboxes
to your parents,
since matches are
not toys.

VANITY

Glue together the two matchboxes side by side and onto the top of the larger box. Stick your faucet between the two matchboxes with a little glue. Then glue on two beads on the left and right of the faucet to serve as handles. Finally, make the sink by gluing the creamer container underneath the faucet.

Materials
· box
· 2 matchboxes
· small plastic hanger
· colorful paper
· 4 small beads
· creamer container

Tools
· scissors
· glue
· pencil
· paint
· paintbrush
· painting smock

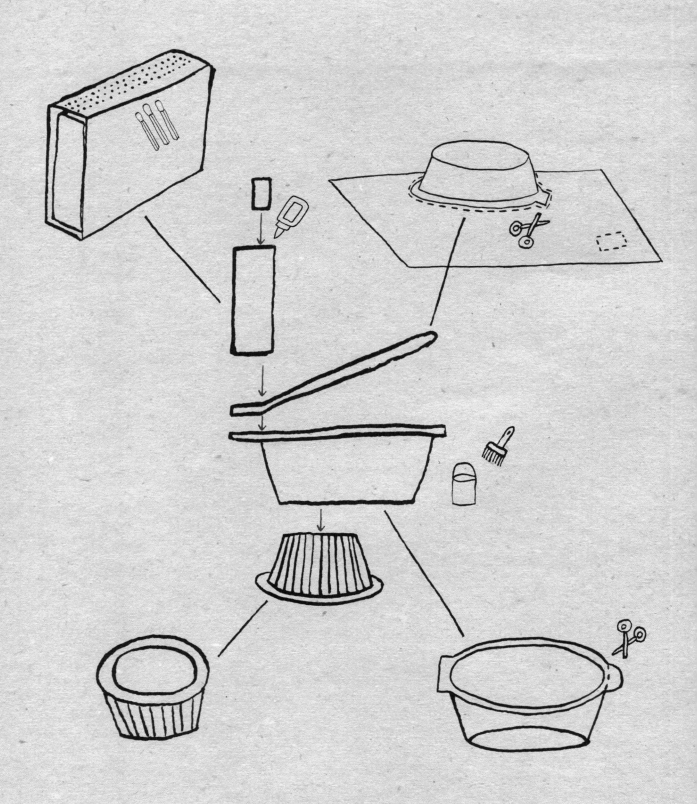

TOILET

Take the plastic bowl and place it on the cardboard with the open side down. Trace the border and cut the shape out from the cardboard. This will be your toilet lid. Now paint the lid, plastic bowl, matchbox, and creamer container in your favorite color. When everything is dry, glue all pieces together, as shown in the picture opposite. Finally, glue a small rectangular piece of paper of a different color to the top of the toilet tank (matchbox) to serve as the flush button. If you like, you can also glue patterned paper onto the toilet lid.

You often get small creamers in a café when you order a hot drink. Check if there are any empty creamers on the tables the next time and take them with you.

Materials
· small plastic bowl
· cardboard
· matchbox
· creamer container
· colorful paper

Tools
· scissors
· glue
· pencil
· paint
· paintbrush
· painting smock

BATHTUB

Paint the inside of the cream cheese
container in a color of your choice.
To decorate the outside of the bathtub,
cut out a narrow strip of giftwrap in the
height and width of your cream cheese
container. You can also use a strip from
a pretty and colorful plastic bag and glue
it to the outside of your bathtub; then it
won't matter if you actually fill it with
water and there is some splashing while
you are playing.

SHOWER PIPE

Cut your drinking straw at the top and
bottom ends so that the shower pipe
is a size that fits the bathtub. Then fold
over the flexible end of the straw and
glue a button to the tip as the shower
head. Finally, glue the pipe to the inside
of the bathtub.

Materials

- cream cheese container
- giftwrap or colorful plastic bag
- flexible drinking straw
- 2 buttons
- cable clamp
- 2 small beads

Tools

- scissors
- glue
- pencil
- adhesive tape
- paint
- paintbrush
- painting smock

FAUCET

Use a cable clamp to make your faucet. Poke the nail that is on the bottom of the cable clamp through the edge of the bathtub. If that is too hard for you to do, you can also just glue the clamp on without the nail. If the clamp is still too wobbly, fasten it with tape. Glue a bead on either side of the cable clamp to serve as faucet handles.

DRAIN

Use the second button to make the bathtub drain. Simply glue it to the bottom of the tub.

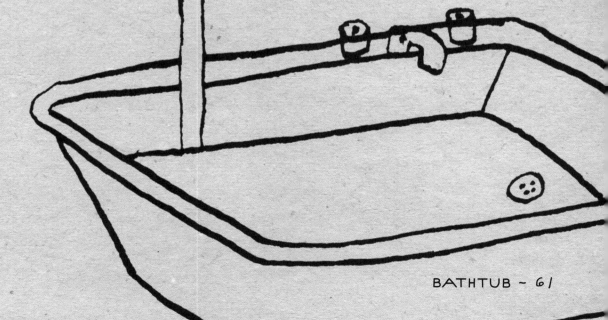

HANGING SHELVES

Draw two rectangular shelves and two rounded side panels on your piece of cardboard and cut them out. Now paint the pieces of cardboard in your favorite color. When everything is dry, place the two side panels next to each other and draw a straight line over both panels where you want to have the first shelf. This way, you can be sure that your shelf will be straight. Do the same thing for the second shelf. Take your scissors and make a slit in the cardboard where the lines are. Now you can stick the shelves into the side panels. If they are still a little too wobbly, put some glue in the slits to make them more stable. Finally, glue the shelves where you want them to go on your wall.

Materials
· cardboard

Tools
· scissors
· glue
· pencil
· paint
· paintbrush
· painting smock

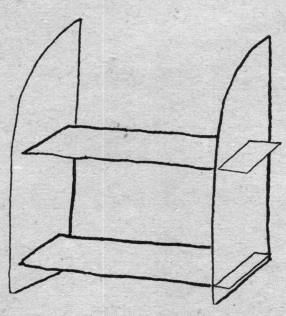

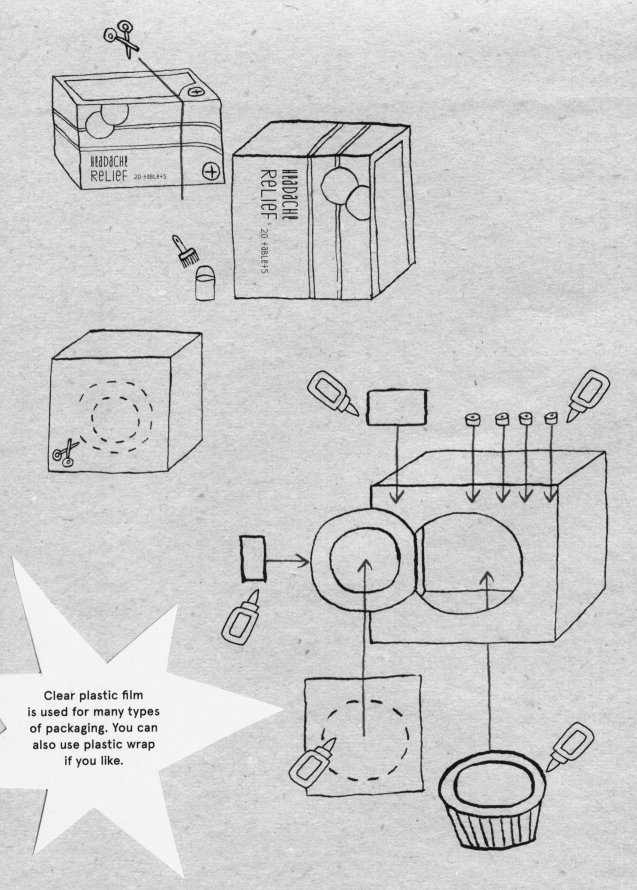

Clear plastic film
is used for many types
of packaging. You can
also use plastic wrap
if you like.

WASHING MACHINE

First cut your box to size. Take an oblong, rectangular box and cut off one end so that it resembles the shape and size of a washing machine. Through the opening you have made you will later be able to insert the washing drum from below. Paint the box in a color of your choice.

When the paint is dry, carefully cut out a circle-shaped door on the front side of the box. Make sure to leave a hinge for the door and use the creamer container as a size guide. Then cut a circle-shaped hole into the door and glue a matching piece of clear plastic film over it from the inside. Now you have a washing machine door with a window.

DETERGENT DRAWER, BUTTONS, & DRUM

Cut two small rectangles out of the construction paper. Glue one to the edge of the door to serve as a handle. The other piece is the detergent dispenser. Glue it to the upper left of the front side of the washing machine. The four beads are the buttons and go on the upper right of the front side. Finally, make a drum with the creamer container by gluing it to the door opening from the inside of the box.

Materials
· box
· clear plastic film
· colored construction paper
· 4 small beads
· creamer container

Tools
· scissors
· glue
· pencil
· paint
· paintbrush
· painting smock

TEENAGER'S BEDROOM

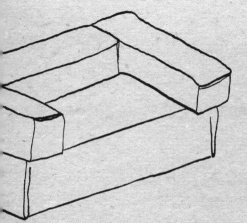

TEENAGER'S BEDROOM

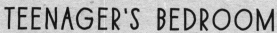

BUILDING
INSTRUCTIONS

Back panel

Side panel

Side panel

Materials
- box
- cardboard

Tools
- scissors or X-Acto knife
- glue
- pencil
- cutting board
- paint
- paintbrush
- painting smock
- adhesive tape

Be careful not to cut yourself when cutting out the bed railings with the X-Acto knife. Ask your mother or father to help you.

DAYBED

For the base of your bed, paint the box (a cornstarch box, for example) in a color of your choice and let it dry.

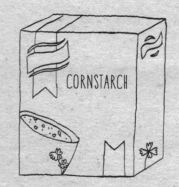

RAILINGS

Place your box on the cardboard on its side and trace your pencil around it. Now you know how tall the lower part of your side panel must be. Next draw the pattern for your railing above this traced part. You can come up with your own patterns or use mine as a template.

Now comes the tricky part: the railing has to be cut out with an X-Acto knife. To do this, place the cardboard with the drawing on a cutting board from your kitchen and cut out the inner areas of your pattern with the X-Acto knife. Make sure to be careful because the knife is very sharp and you can easily slip. If you don't have an X-Acto knife, you can also just paint your railings on the cardboard and cut only along the outer edge. This way you will still have a railing, but you don't have to cut out any holes.

Once you have finished the two sides and the back, you can glue the lower parts of the three panels to your painted box. Use small strips of clear tape to connect the left and right side railings to the back.

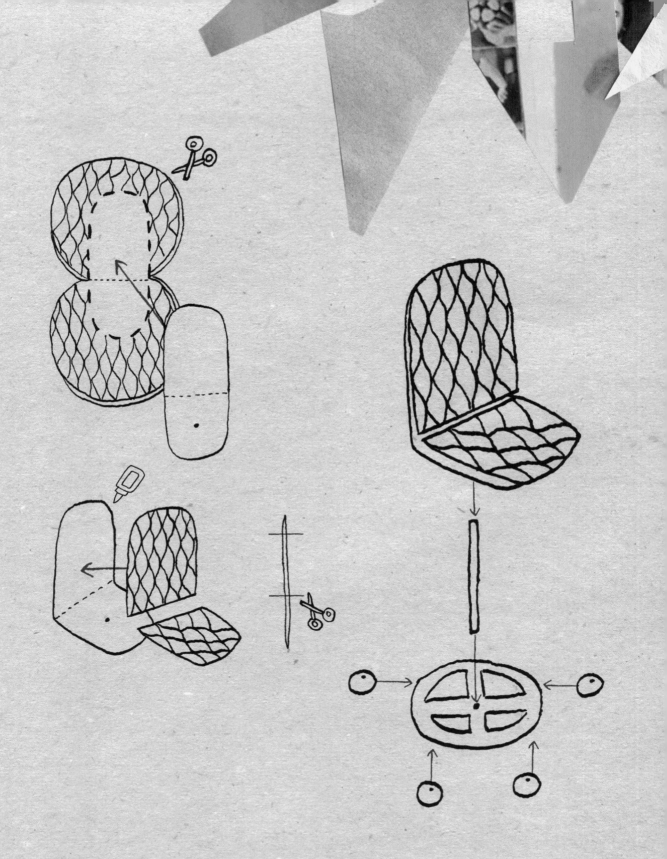

CHAIR SEAT & CUSHION

Take the cardboard and draw an elongated oval shape, like the shape of a large band-aid, on it. This will be the seat of your desk chair. Once you have cut out this shape, place it on the two cotton pads, trace the shape, and cut out the cotton pads. Now bend the cardboard seat surface as shown above left and glue the two pieces of cotton onto it.

Materials
- cardboard
- 2 cotton pads
- 4 medium beads
- toothpick

Tools
- scissors
- glue
- X-Acto knife
- pencil
- awl

COLUMN & BASE

To make the base of your desk chair, take your cardboard again and draw a circle on it with a cross in the middle. With the X-Acto knife cut out the resulting four "cake slices" and glue the four beads onto the bottom to serve as caster wheels.

The toothpick will be the column that connects the seat and the base. Cut the ends off so the column is an appropriate height. Then take your awl and make a hole in the middle of the cross and in the middle of the seat. Next glue all of the parts together as shown in the picture opposite.

DISPLAY CABINET
& SHELVES

For your display cabinet, you need two different-sized boxes. Use the pictures below as a guideline for the sizes needed. For the two cabinet tops and two shelves, cut rectangular shapes out of the cardboard, using the boxes as guidelines. Then paint the boxes and boards all in the same color.

When everything is dry, mark where the doors are supposed to go in your top cabinet. The dotted lines in the picture opposite show you where to cut. Do the same for the bottom cabinet. Make sure to be very careful when using your X-Acto knife or scissors, because you can easily slip and cut your finger. Now take the eight fuse beads and glue everything together, as shown on the facing page.

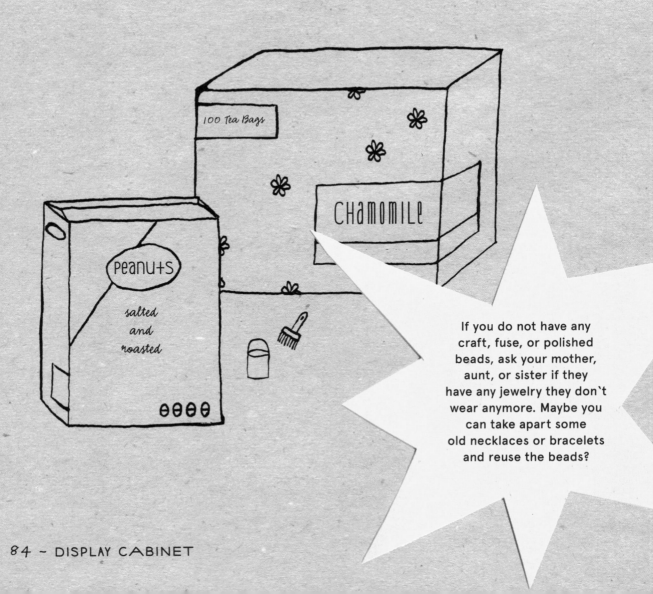

If you do not have any craft, fuse, or polished beads, ask your mother, aunt, or sister if they have any jewelry they don't wear anymore. Maybe you can take apart some old necklaces or bracelets and reuse the beads?

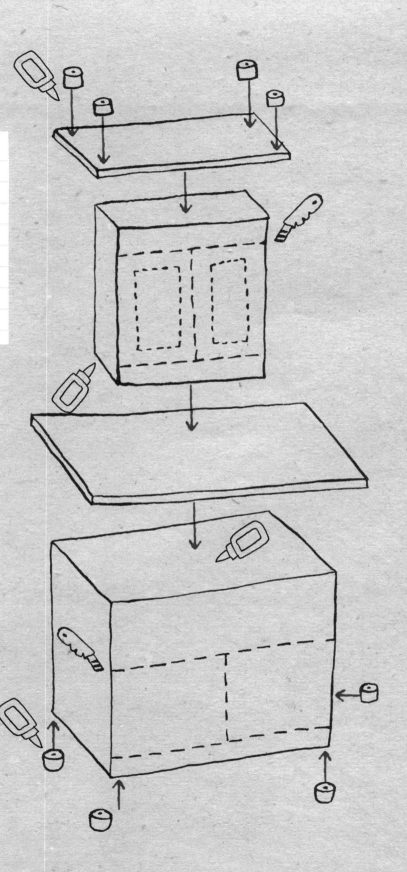

Materials
- 2 boxes
- cardboard
- 8 fuse beads
- clear plastic film
- paper
- 6 polished beads

Tools
- scissors
- glue
- X-Acto knife
- pencil
- paint
- paintbrush
- painting smock

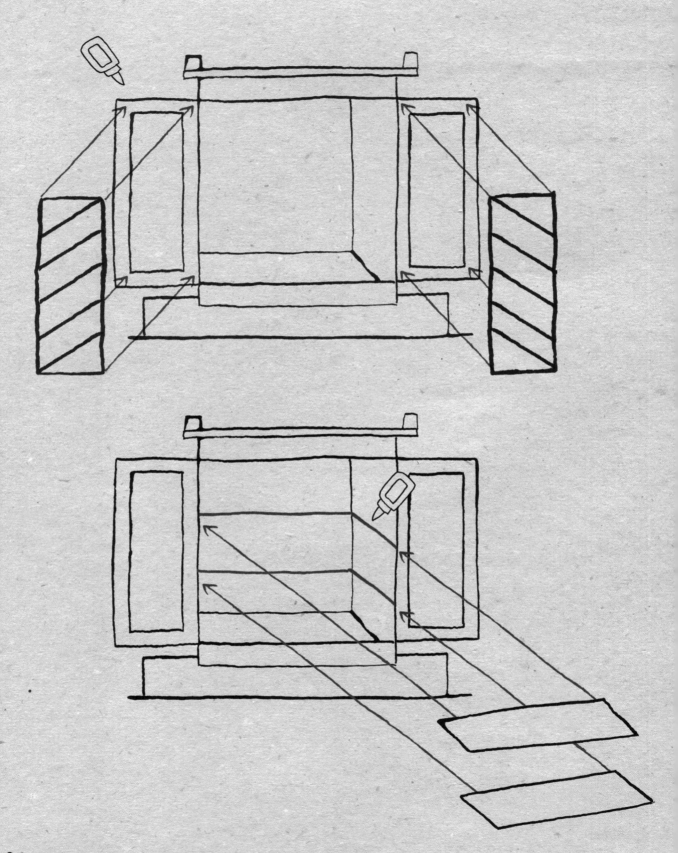

86 ~ DISPLAY CABINET

CABINET DOORS
& KNOBS

While the glue on your display cabinet is drying, cut out two pieces of clear plastic film about the same size as the doors of your top cabinet. Now carefully open the doors and brush some glue onto the inner frame of the doors. Then stick on the pieces of plastic film, as shown in the top picture on the opposite page. Next glue the shelves into the top cabinet.

Take a piece of paper, cut out two small rectangles, and glue them to your bottom cabinet, as shown in the picture below, to represent drawers. As the very last step, make door and drawer knobs by gluing six pretty polished beads onto the doors of the top cabinet, the center of the "pretend" drawers, and the doors of the bottom cabinet.

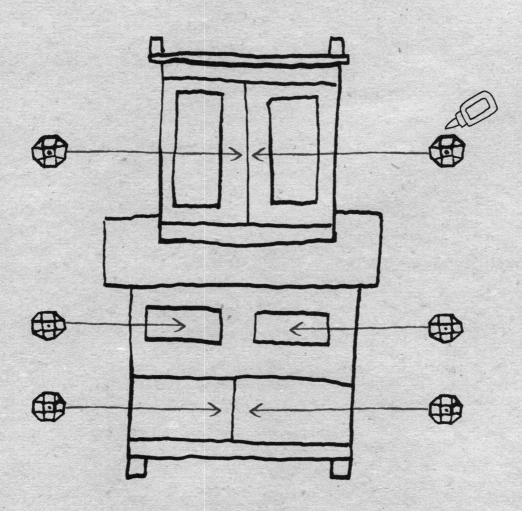

ARMCHAIR NO. 2

First take the sponge and cut out three long pieces, which will serve as the back and arms of your armchair. Then wrap each of the three sponge pieces and the box (seat) like a present in the felt and glue the edges closed, as shown on the facing page. Finally, glue the three sponge pieces onto your box.

Materials
· box
· sponge
· felt or fabric scraps

Tools
· scissors
· glue

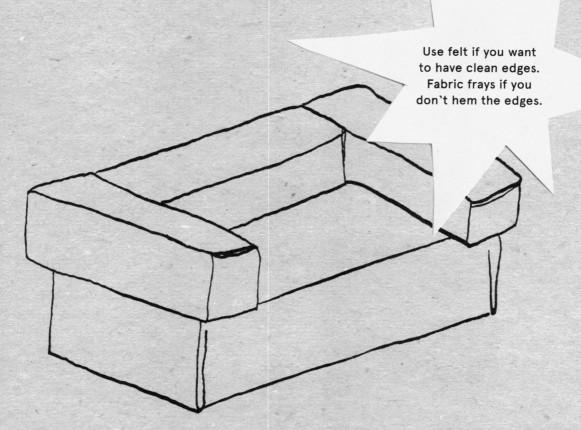

Use felt if you want to have clean edges. Fabric frays if you don't hem the edges.

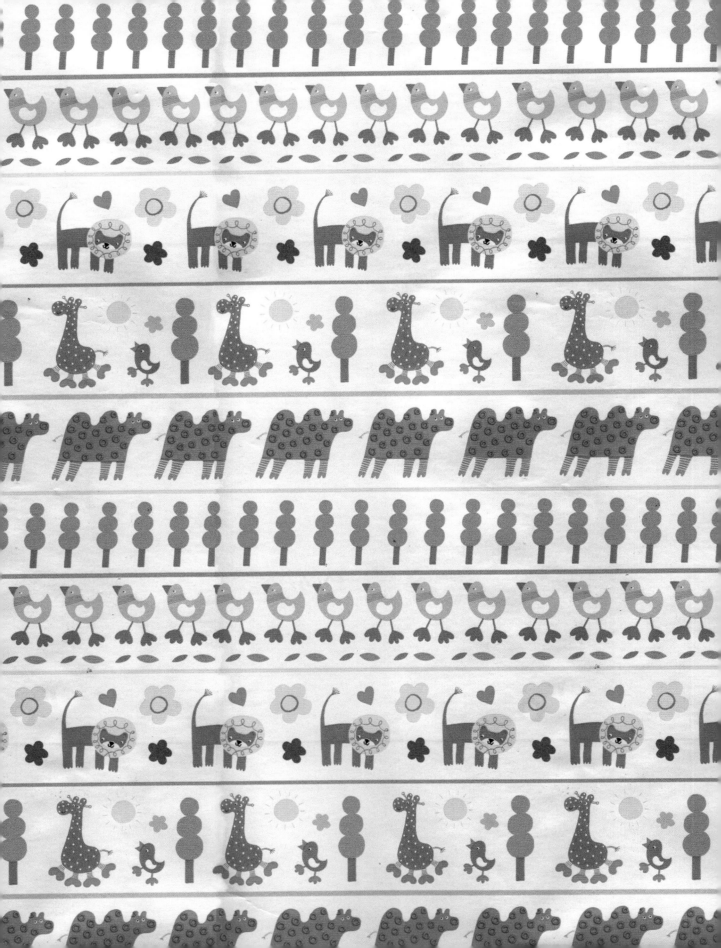

CHILDREN'S BEDROOM

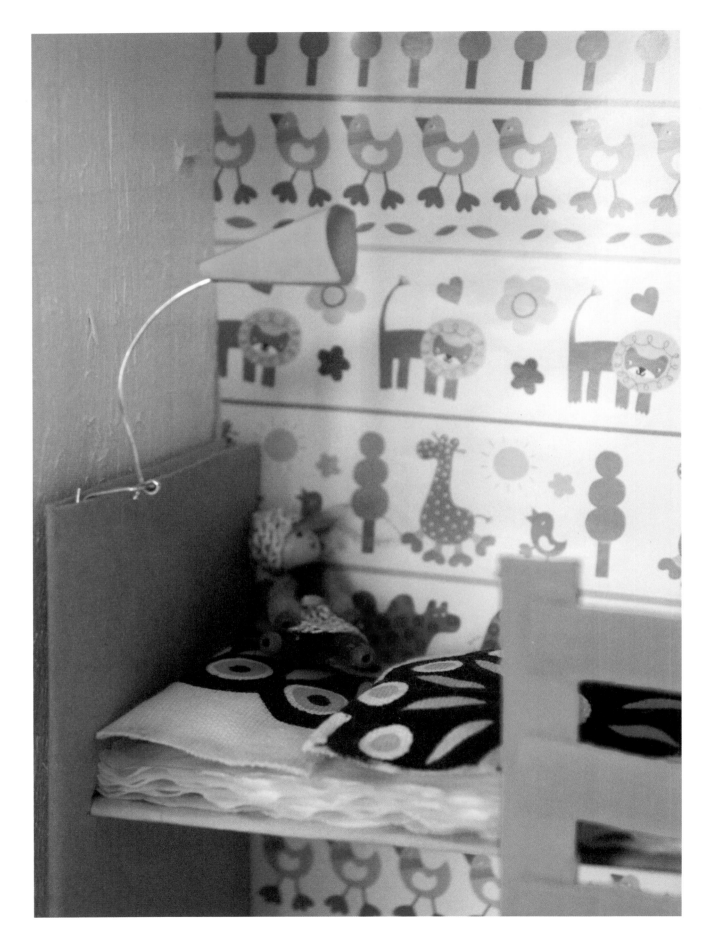

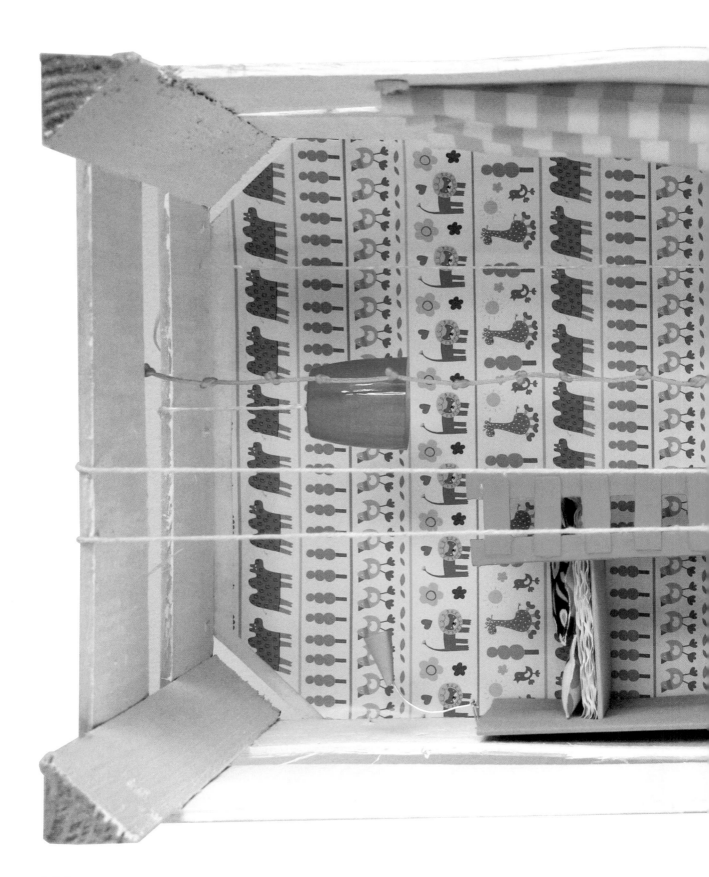

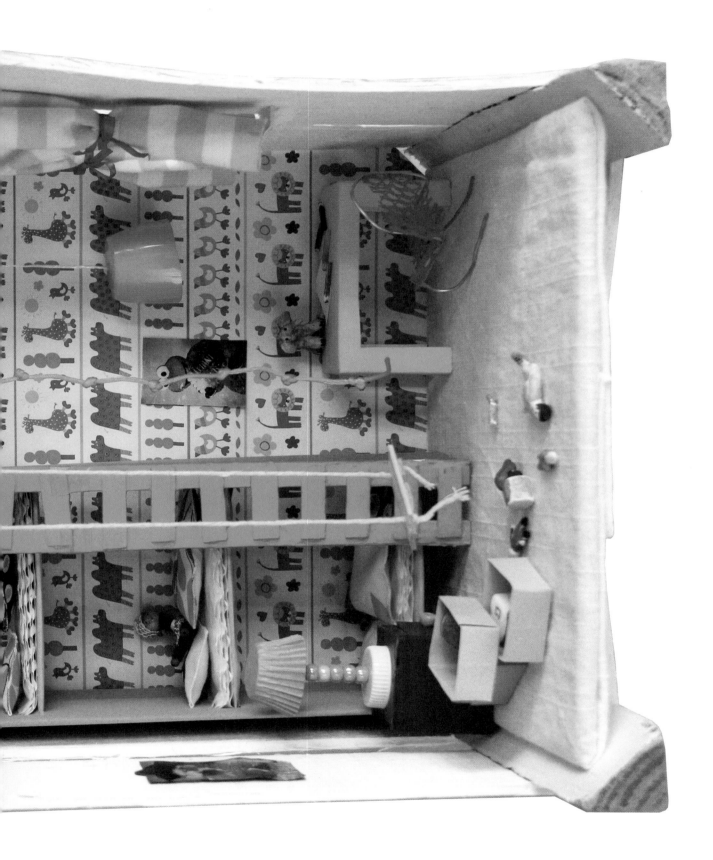

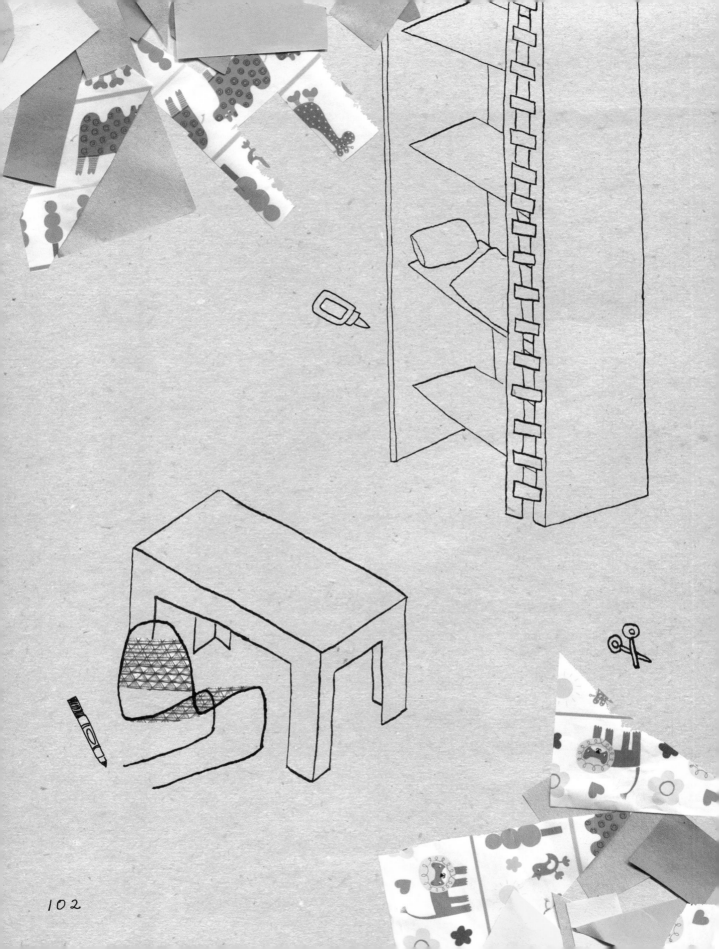

CHILDREN'S BEDROOM

BUILDING
INSTRUCTIONS

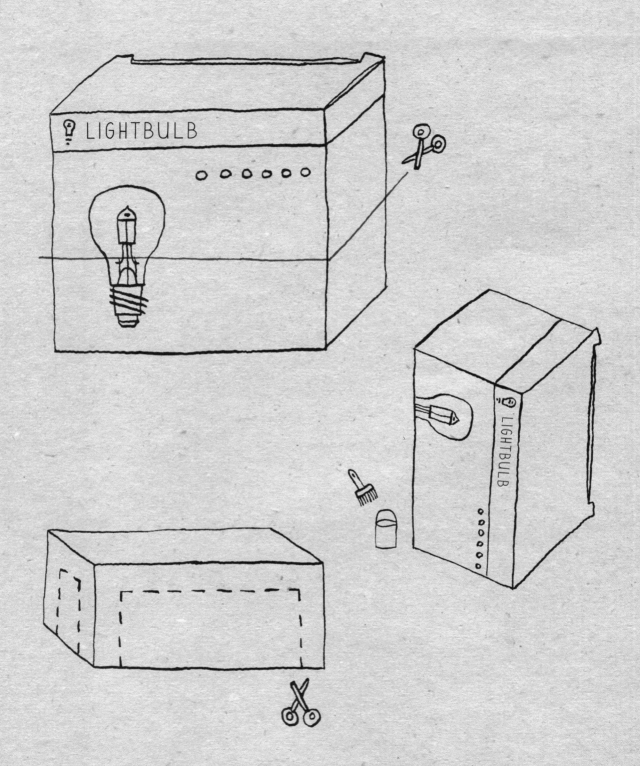

DESK

First, cut off the lower part of your box (along the red line in the top picture opposite). Then paint the rest of the box inside and out. The paint will make the desk more stable. After it is dry, cut out a rectangle shape on all four sides of your box to make the legs (bottom picture opposite). Now your desk is finished!

You can find instructions for making the desk chair on pages 172–73.

You can find instructions for making the desk chair on pages 172–73.

Materials
· box

Tools
· scissors
· pencil
· paint
· paintbrush
· painting smock

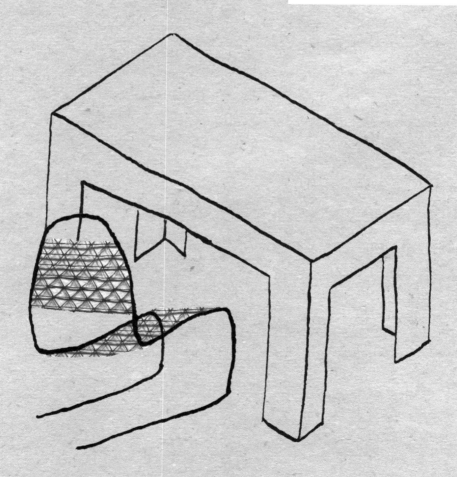

For the lamp stand
you need beads
with a large hole
so that they fit on
the toothpick.
Color your lampshade
with markers,
if you like.

LAMP NO. 1

With the awl, bore a hole into the center of the crown cap. Drip a little glue into the hole and insert the toothpick. Now "string" your beads onto the toothpick. If your toothpick is too long, cut it to size and put some glue on the last bead. Now overturn the creamer container and stick it to the last bead to make the lamp shade. Make sure to let everything dry completely before you play with it.

Materials
· crown cap
· 5–8 beads
· toothpick
· creamer container

Tools
· glue
· awl

BUNK BED

Take a large piece of cardboard (from a shoebox, for example) and cut out two long rectangles of the same size. These will be the side panels of your bunk bed. The more bunks you want it to have, the taller the sides must be. Now cut out four smaller rectangles for the beds. Glue colorful paper onto all of your cardboard pieces, or wrap them like a present and stick the edges together with adhesive tape.

Next place the side panels side by side, take your ruler, and make a mark on both pieces at the height at which the first bed is supposed to go. Repeat this for all of your beds. Then carefully cut slits into the side panels where you marked them with an X-Acto knife. Now you can put a little glue in the slots and insert the beds.

You can make pillows and quilts for your beds the same way you made the sofa cushions (back and arm rests) on pages 38–39.

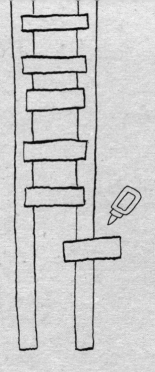

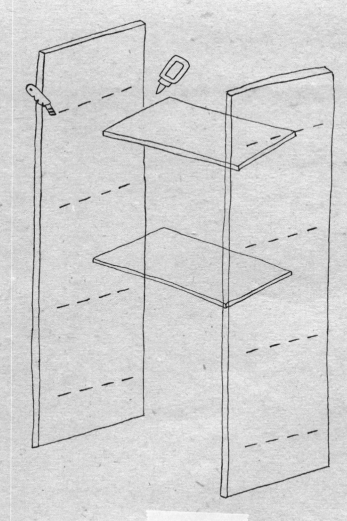

LADDER

Cut two narrow strips and several small rectangles out of your cardboard. Then glue the small pieces (the rungs) onto the two long strips. When everything is completely dry, coat your ladder with paint and let it dry again. Finally, glue the ladder onto the front of your bunkbed, as shown in the picture opposite.

Materials
· cardboard
· colorful paper

Tools
· ruler
· pencil
· scissors
· X-Acto knife
· glue
· paint
· paintbrush
· painting smock
· adhesive tape

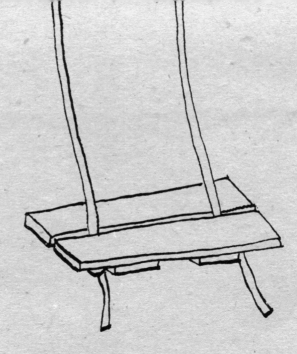

SWING

To make the seat, take one of your popsicle sticks and cut off the rounded ends. Then cut it in half to get two pieces of the same length. From the second popsicle stick, cut out two smaller pieces. Now place your larger wood pieces next to each other, leaving a small gap, and glue the smaller popsicle pieces on top as connectors. Let the swing seat dry completely. Then take the parcel string and cut off two long pieces of the same length. Insert the two strings through the gap in the seat outside the connectors and knot the string on the underside, as shown on the page opposite. Double or triple the knots if necessary. To finish your swing, glue the upper ends of the strings to the ceiling of your children's bedroom.

Materials
· 2 popsicle sticks
· parcel string

Tools
· scissors
· glue
· pencil

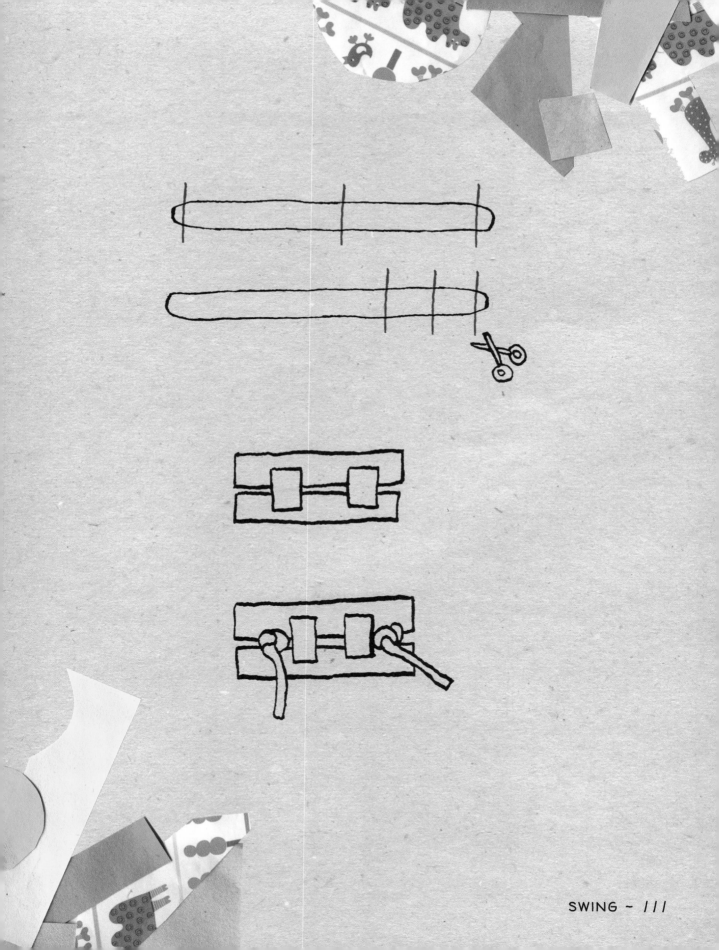

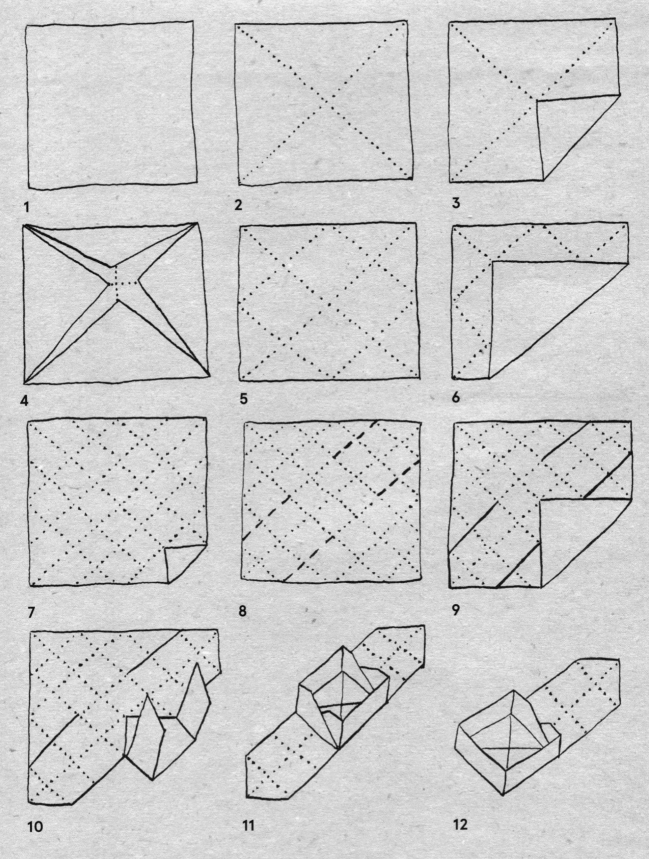

1

2

3

4

5

6

7

8

9

10

11

12

BOX

1 Take a sheet of square paper and place it in front of you.

2 Fold the paper diagonally from both sides and then unfold it.

3, **4**, and **5** Fold all four corners into the middle. Then unfold the paper again.

6 Now fold each corner to the farthest fold line opposite and unfold it again.

7 Then fold each corner to the closest fold line and back again.

8 Cut along the dotted lines, as shown in the picture.

9 and **10** If you now fold one of the non-cut corners to the center and then fold up the resulting side parts and fold them forward, you have the first inner wall of your box.

11 Repeat this on the opposite side.

12 Fold the two remaining pieces over the side walls, and the box is finished.

Materials
· square piece of paper

Tools
· scissors

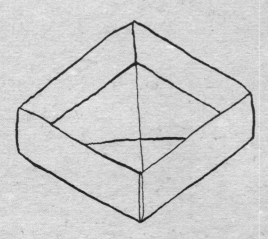

BOX ~ 113

KITCHEN

120

KITCHEN

- -

BUILDING
INSTRUCTIONS

- -

STOVE & OVEN DOOR

Take a small square box (from a face cream, for example) and paint it a pretty color. Paint the top side white so that the stovetop stands out from the rest of the unit. When the paint is dry, use an X-Acto knife or scissors to cut out the oven door on the dotted line in the center, as shown above. Fold back the cut piece to open your oven door.

HANDLE & KNOBS

Now glue the small beads onto the front side of the stove to serve as knobs. With pliers, bend a small piece of wire into the shape of an elongated handle and stick it through the oven door. Glue the points of the wire to the inside of the oven door. To make the handle more secure and to reduce the risk of poking yourself, you can also glue small pieces of fabric over the ends of the wire.

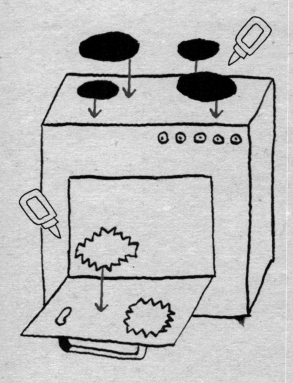

BURNERS

Now cut four circles of various sizes out of the black construction paper. These will be the burners. If you have a hard time making round circles, trace around some coins to help you. Finally, glue the black burners onto the top of the box.

Materials
· box
· 5 small beads
· wire
· fabric scraps
· black construction paper

Tools
· scissors
· X-Acto knife
· glue
· pencil
· paint
· paintbrush
· painting smock
· pliers

BUCKET

For your bucket, you need a large plastic cap (for example, the cap of a bottle of mouthwash or liquid laundry detergent). Tie a piece of parcel string around the cap, make a secure double knot, and cut off the ends. Then take another piece of string and knot the ends to the already fastened string on opposite sides of the bucket, leaving some slack. Now your bucket has a handle.

MOP

To make the fringe for your mop, cut off eight pieces of yarn of the same length and one piece of yarn that is a little bit longer. Place the longer piece horizontally on the table and lay the eight other pieces on top of it crosswise. Now wrap the longer piece of yarn around the shorter pieces and tie them together. Fold the top fringes over the bottom fringes, put a drop of glue on top of the nub, and insert the skewer through the hole. Then cut off another long piece of yarn and wrap it tightly around the fringe bundle with the skewer. Tie it with a knot and cut off the ends.

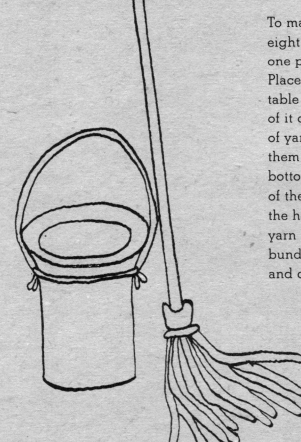

mouthwash
fresh & minty

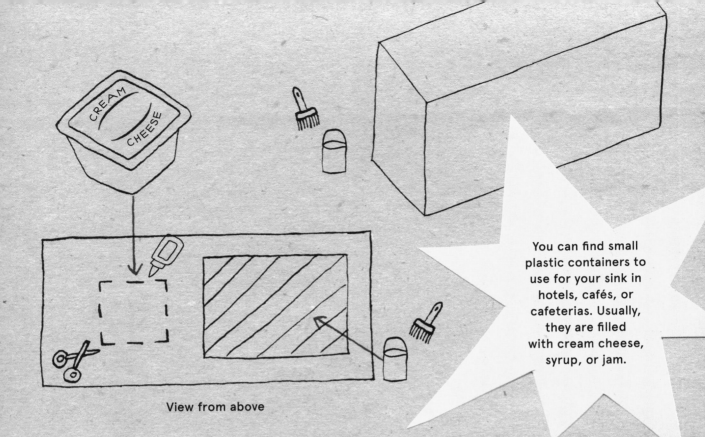

View from above

SINK & DRAINING BOARD

First paint the box in a color of your choice. When it is dry, take your small plastic container and place it on top of the painted box. Now trace the shape of the container. Cut along the line with scissors to make a hole in which to insert the plastic container. This will be your sink. Before you put in the plastic container, brush a little glue on the edge of the cut-out hole. Next to the sink, you can paint a rectangular area white, like the shaded area shown in the picture above, to represent the draining board for the dishes.

CABINET DOORS & FAUCET

Now draw a sideways H on the front of your sink unit, as shown in the top picture opposite, and cut along the lines with an X-Acto knife. Fold back the cut pieces to open your cabinet doors. Now glue a bead onto the left and right doors to serve as knobs. Finally, take your cable clamp and stick its nail through the top of the cabinet behind the sink to make the faucet, and glue the beads to the right and left as handles.

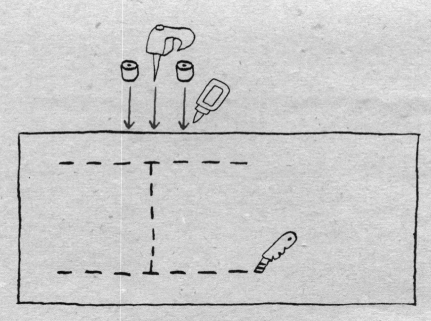

View from the front

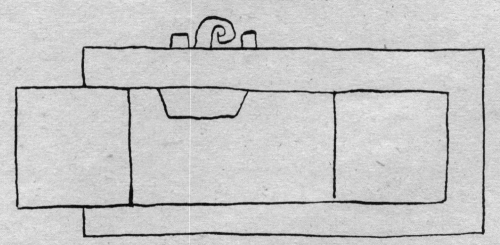

Materials
· box
· small plastic container
· 4 beads
· cable clamp

Tools
· scissors
· X-Acto knife
· glue
· pencil
· paint
· paintbrush
· painting smock

REFRIGERATOR
DOORS & HANDLES

First make sure that the inside of your drink carton is clean: fill it with some water through the straw hole, hold the hole closed, shake the carton, and squeeze the water back out. Then paint the drink carton a color of your choice. When it is dry, cut out two refrigerator doors with the X-Acto knife as shown in the picture below, and fold back the cut pieces to open your refrigerator doors.

To make the handles for the doors, snip off two small pieces of wire and bend them into a handle shape with pliers. With the awl, poke four holes into the two doors and insert the wire into the holes. Then glue small scraps of fabric over the wire ends on the inside of the refrigerator door to prevent getting poked.

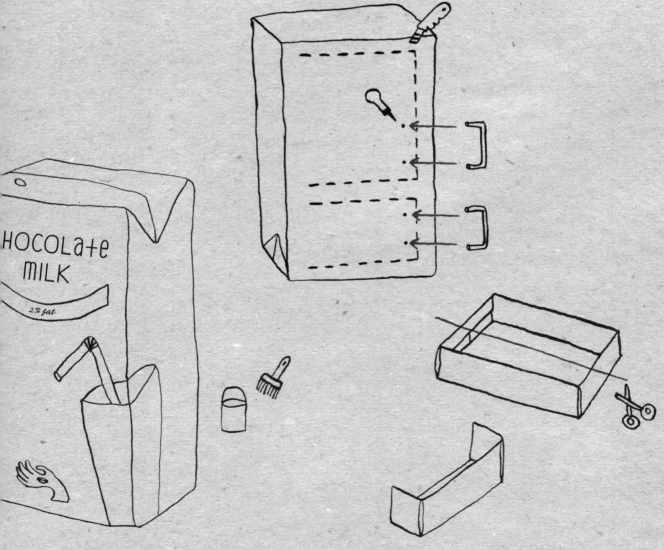

Materials

- drink carton
- wire
- fabric scraps
- matchbox drawer
- cardboard

Tools

- scissors
- glue
- X-Acto knife
- pencil
- paint
- paintbrush
- painting smock
- awl
- pliers

BEVERAGE RACK & SHELVES

To make the beverage rack, take the matchbox drawer, cut it in half lengthwise, and glue one half to the inside of the upper refrigerator door.

From the cardboard, cut out two shelves. The easiest way to figure out the right size for the shelves is to trace around the drink carton with a pencil. Now carefully put some glue on the edges of your shelves and glue them to the inside of your refrigerator.

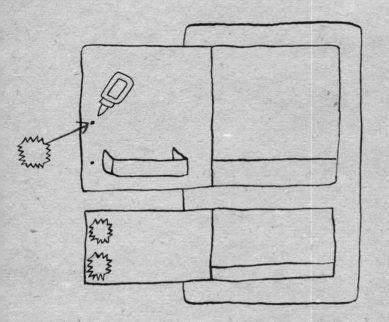

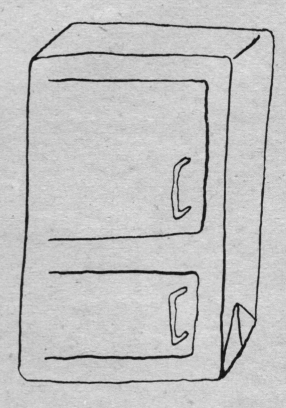

RADIO

First paint the block of wood whatever color you want. Now take some construction paper and cut out a long, narrow piece as a carrying handle and snip a piece from your wire for the antenna. When the wood is dry, make a hole in the top using your awl and insert the wire antenna together with a little glue. Glue one bead on the very top of the antenna and the other four onto the front side of your radio to make knobs. Then glue the paper handle next to the antenna, leaving a gap as shown. And finally, take the marker and draw the tape deck and speakers on the front of your radio.

You can get all kinds of wood scraps for free in hardware stores. Just ask a salesperson if you can have some.

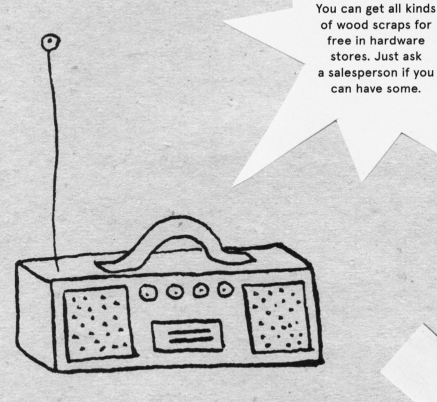

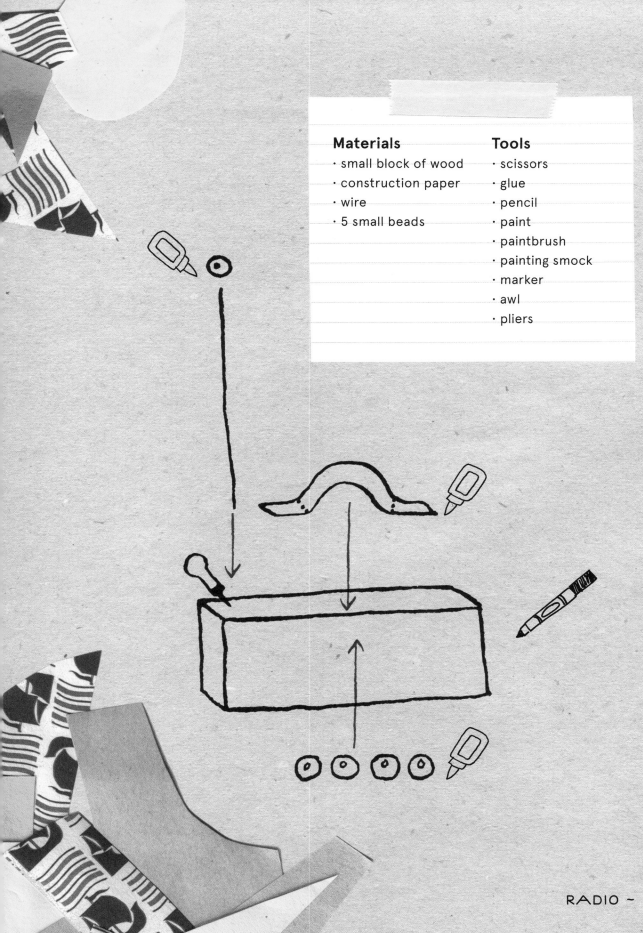

Materials
- small block of wood
- construction paper
- wire
- 5 small beads

Tools
- scissors
- glue
- pencil
- paint
- paintbrush
- painting smock
- marker
- awl
- pliers

BEDROOM

142

BEDROOM

BUILDING INSTRUCTIONS

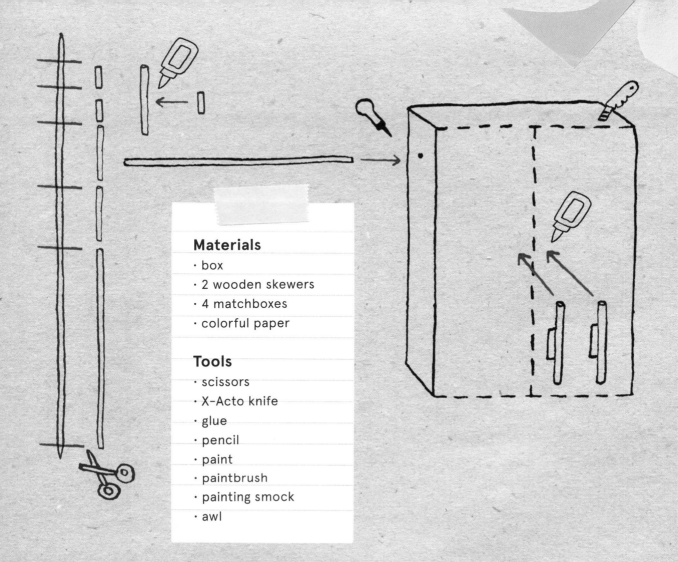

Materials
· box
· 2 wooden skewers
· 4 matchboxes
· colorful paper

Tools
· scissors
· X-Acto knife
· glue
· pencil
· paint
· paintbrush
· painting smock
· awl

CLOTHES ROD & DOOR HANDLES

First cut a long piece from the skewer to match the width of your box. This will be your clothes rod. From the other skewer, cut two medium-sized and two small pieces. To make the two door handles of your wardrobe, glue a small piece of stick to the center of a medium-sized piece.

WARDROBE

Paint your box in a color of your choice and let it dry. Then cut along the dotted line with an X-Acto knife, as shown in the picture above. Using your awl, make two holes on both sides of your wardrobe at the top and insert the clothes rod through the holes. Now glue the door handles on the outside of the two wardrobe doors.

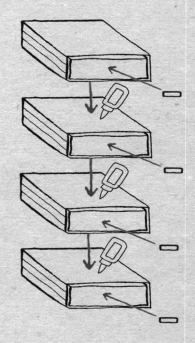

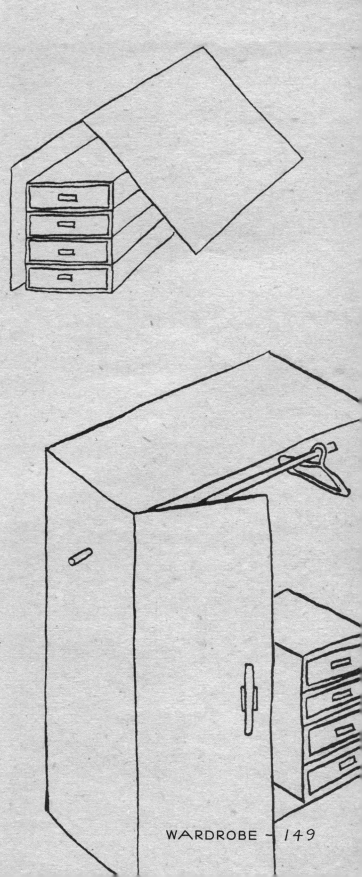

DRAWER CABINET

Glue four matchboxes on top of one another. Cut four small pieces from the remaining skewer and glue one small piece on each of the inner parts of the matchboxes to make handles for your drawers. To make your cabinet look nicer, you can glue some colorful paper to its top and sides. Finally, glue the drawer cabinet into your wardrobe.

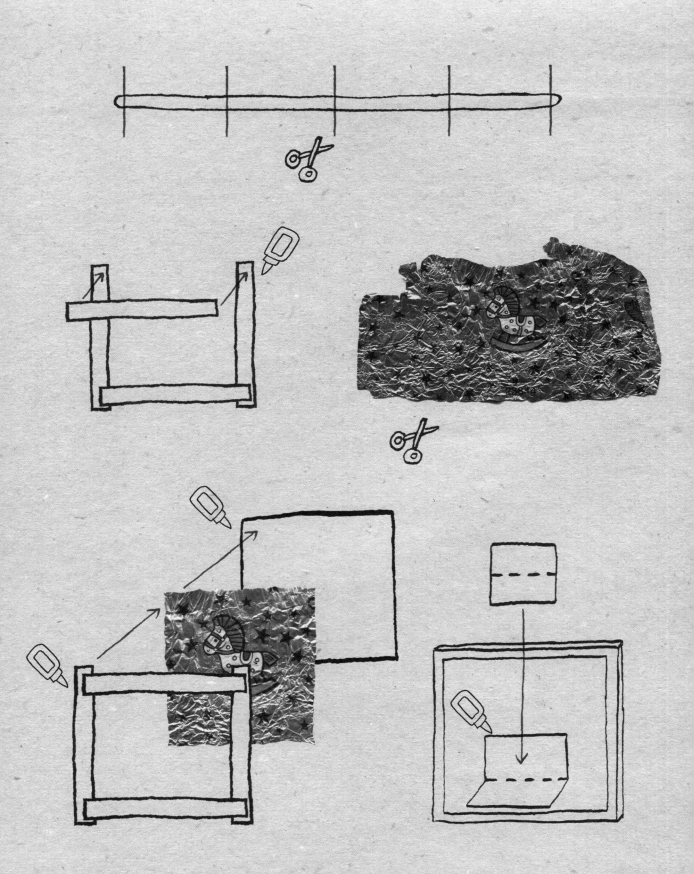

PICTURE FRAME

Take your wooden stick and cut it into four pieces of equal length, first cutting off any rounded tips. Now glue the four pieces of wood together to make a square frame. Then take a pretty foil candy wrapper and some cardboard and cut both into squares of the same size. Glue the candy wrapper to the cardboard. Then glue your wooden frame onto the candy wrapper. Now cut out a somewhat smaller piece of rectangular cardboard. Fold it in half and glue it to the back of your picture frame as a frame stand. Let everything dry completely before you put up your picture frame.

Materials
- narrow wooden stick (for example, coffee stirrer)
- foil candy wrapper or magazine clipping
- cardboard

Tools
- scissors
- glue
- pencil

The wooden stick you need for the picture frame looks like a narrow popsicle stick. You sometimes get such sticks instead of a spoon for stirring a hot drink in a café or at a bakery.

CRADLE

First take the small plastic container and poke four holes into the bottom. Now cut the skewers into four pieces of the same length, drip a little glue into the holes, and insert the sticks into the holes. While the glue dries, take the wire and bend it into an L shape. Next make a hole in the rim of your plastic container, put a drop of glue into it, and stick the bent wire in the hole. Take a small old crocheted blanket or a nice piece of fabric, cut it to size, and glue it around the edge of the plastic container. Then cut out a rectangular piece of fabric and tie it together on both ends with the satin ribbon. This is the canopy for your cradle. Put it over the wire rod.

Materials
- small plastic container
- 2 wooden skewers
- wire
- scraps of fabric or small crocheted blanket
- satin ribbon

Tools
- awl
- glue
- scissors

When you buy a new T-shirt, there are often loops of satin ribbon sewn inside. You can cut these off and use them for your canopy.

CRADLE ~ 153

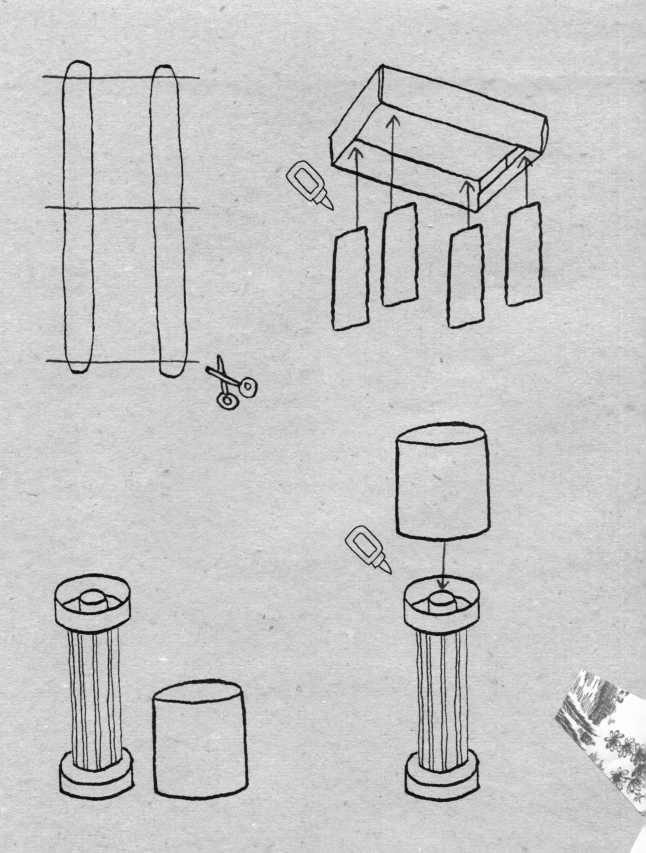

BEDSIDE TABLE

Take your popsicle sticks and cut off the rounded ends. Then cut the two sticks into four equal pieces, which will be your table legs. Glue the legs into the matchbox drawer as shown on the facing page. If you like, you can paint your little bedside table in a pretty color or glue colorful paper on it.

LAMP NO. 2

For your lampshade, find a nice plastic lid (for example, from a small travel-sized shampoo). Now simply glue this lid on the yarn bobbin and your lamp is finished.

Materials
- 2 popsicle sticks
- matchbox drawer
- plastic lid
- empty plastic yarn bobbin

Tools
- scissors
- glue
- pencil

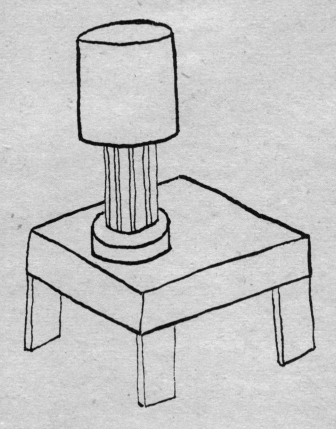

If you want your bed to have a mattress, you can use honeycomb paper to make one. Honeycomb paper is often used for protection in boxes of chocolate.

DOUBLE BED

Take the cardboard and cut out a head- and footboard for your bed. Make sure their widths match the width of your box. Now paint the box and the two cut-out pieces of cardboard in the same color. When everything is dry, glue the cardboard parts to the box.

Materials
· cardboard
· box

Tools
· scissors
· glue
· pencil
· paint
· paintbrush
· painting smock

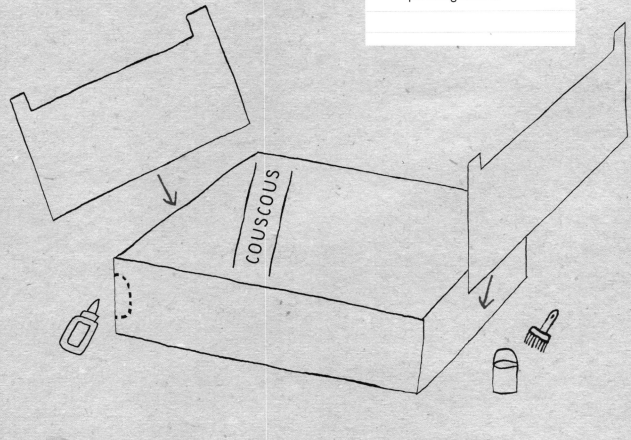

PATIO

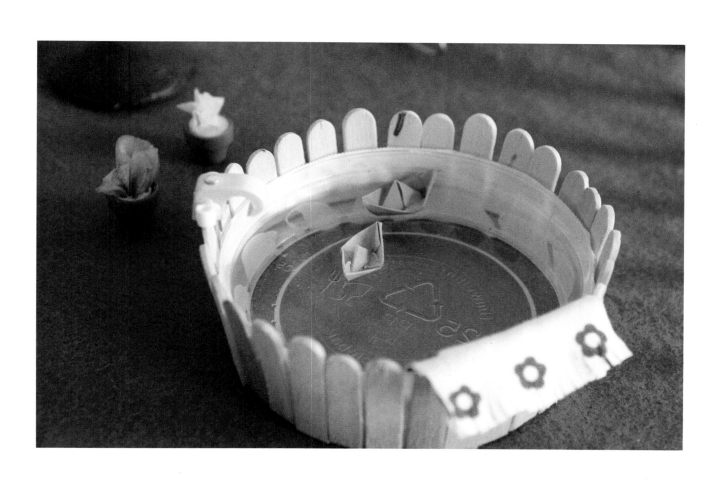

PATIO

- -

BUILDING INSTRUCTIONS

- -

SUN UMBRELLA

Cut off a narrow slice from the cork and stick the four toothpicks into the outer edge as shown in the picture opposite. Now take the parcel string and knot one end tightly to one of the toothpicks very close to the cork. Next stretch the string from toothpick to toothpick by wrapping it around one toothpick and then moving on to the next. Repeat this until you reach the ends of the toothpicks. Knot the string tightly to the end of a toothpick and cut off the rest. Take your beads, put a small drop of glue on the ends of the toothpicks, and glue the beads on. This way, the shade looks prettier, and you can no longer prick yourself on the toothpicks.

Using the awl, poke a hole in the middle of the large plastic lid. Put some glue in the hole and insert your skewer. Before you stick the finished umbrella shade on the other end of the skewer, press the modeling clay into the plastic lid from below. This will make the stand heavier so that the umbrella is stable and does not tip over.

Materials
· cork
· 4 toothpicks
· parcel string
· 4 small beads
· large plastic lid
· wooden skewer
· modeling clay

Tools
· scissors
· X-Acto knife
· glue
· awl

SUN UMBRELLA ~ 169

WHIRLPOOL

For the wood paneling around your whirlpool, cut all of your popsicle sticks in half so that they are the same length and glue them to the outside of the small plastic container, with the rounded ends pointing upward. When everything is completely dry, glue the cable clamp to the wood paneling as the faucet, and to the left and right of it, the beads as the faucet knobs.

Materials
· 15 popsicle sticks
· small plastic container
· cable clamp
· 2 fuse beads

Tools
· scissors
· glue
· pencil

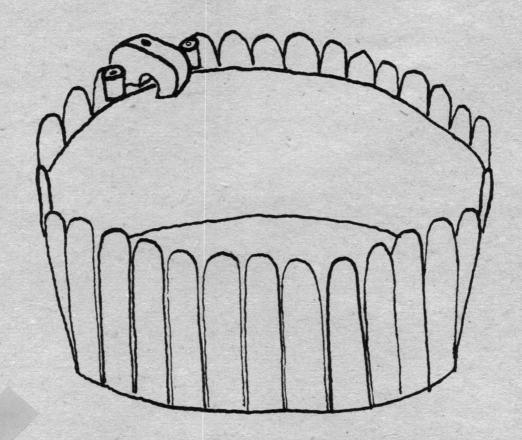

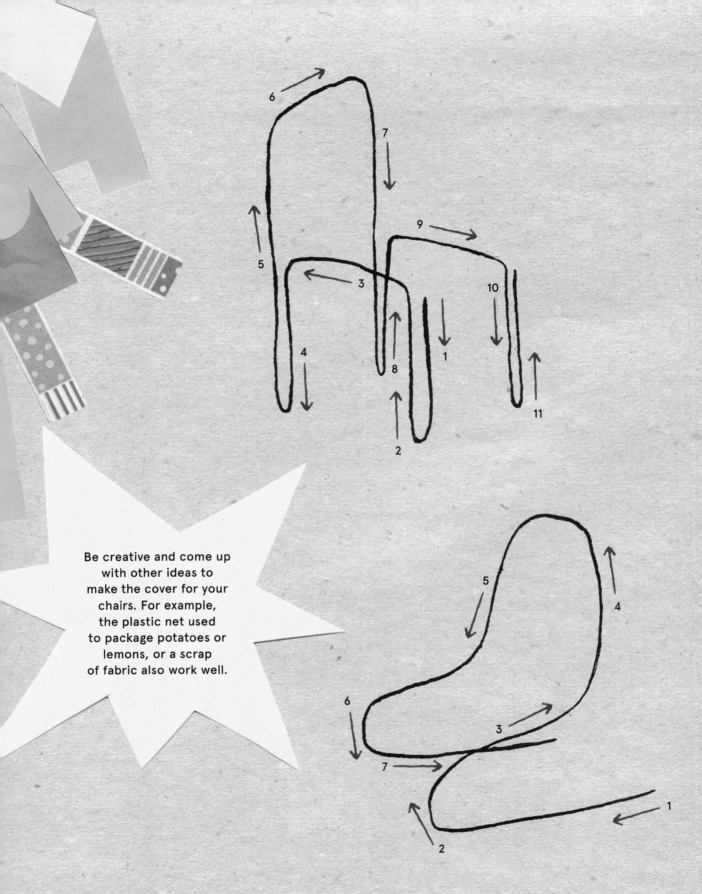

Be creative and come up with other ideas to make the cover for your chairs. For example, the plastic net used to package potatoes or lemons, or a scrap of fabric also work well.

CHAIRS

Materials
· wire
· crepe tape or colorful
  adhesive tape

Tools
· scissors
· pliers

For each chair, take a piece of wire approximately twelve inches long and, using pliers, bend it into whatever chair shape you want. You can bend your chair following steps 1 to 11 in the top picture on the facing page, or as shown in steps 1 to 7 in the bottom picture on the facing page. If the chair is still a little tilted and wobbly, put it on a table and press on it until it stands properly. Cut off any extra wire sticking out with scissors.

Now take some crepe tape or colorful adhesive tape, cut a few pieces to size, and glue them around the wire frame to make the seat and back of your chair.

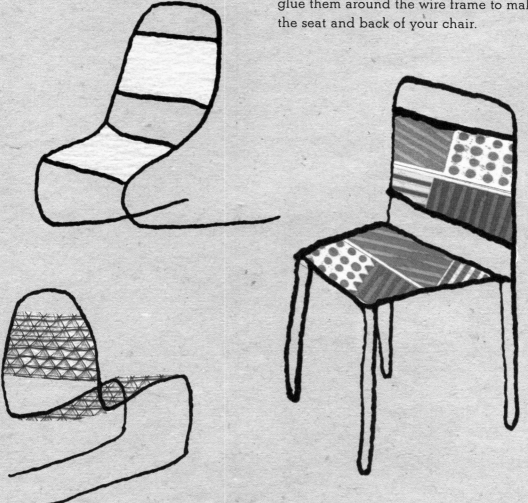

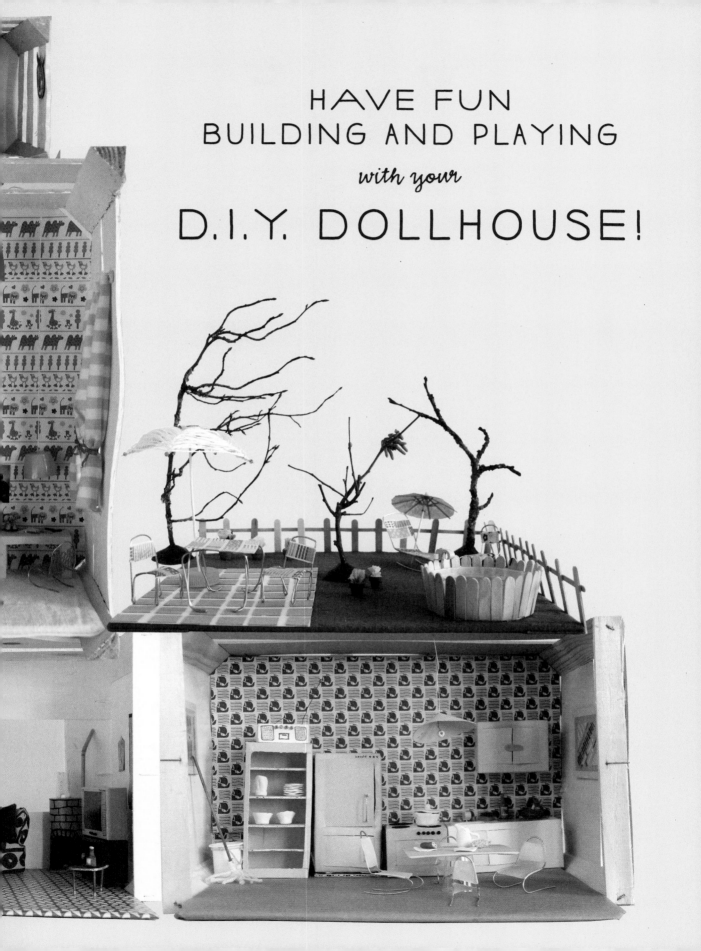

HAVE FUN
BUILDING AND PLAYING
with your
D.I.Y. DOLLHOUSE!

acknowledgments

I would like to thank everyone who helped me realize this book project.

My heartfelt thanks go to Prof. B. Mölck-Tassel and Prof. Dr. M. Diener for their continuous support. In addition to providing assistance with artistic questions, illustration issues, and the text, their constant interest in my work and the many ideas they each brought to it from their different areas of specialization were very helpful.

I especially thank my parents for their patience, involvement, and useful suggestions for the creation of this work, and to all those who contributed to this book, in both small and large ways.

Thank you also to my faithful friends, who have always been there for me, no matter how difficult it has or I have been.

To Ira, who helped me so much with the photos for this book. Without her, the pictures would have only been half as good. And I would never have gone on so many wonderful outings with shopping carts!

To Jana, who made sure the text was orthographically correct and ultimately had to admit that recycling strengthens interpersonal relationships! Olé!

To Ilka, my study partner and chef. Without her many lunches, I would probably have starved at some point.

To Elli, my great job-application assistant! Without her help, I would have written novel-length application letters.

To Tanja & Lisa K., my InDesign experts, who always gave me helpful tips.

A huge thank-you to all those who are not mentioned by name here, but who were always there for me, whether in their thoughts, on the telephone, or in real life, and gave me courage and perseverance.